Pum's Lazy Cuisine

by Yardfon Pum Booranapim

For $\int^2$

Nice to meet you
and
happy cooking

See you
and the BABY
SamusterSoon —

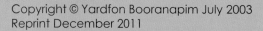

Food preparation and design by Pum

Food photography by *Mr Janez Pukŝiĉ*
Additional photography by *Robert S. Dann* (pages 3, 12, 13) and *Manuel Cortico Dos Santos* (opposite page)

Text by *Pum*
Graphic design by *Ed & Josh Grindall*
Cover design by *Josh Grindall*
Web design by *Josh Grindall*

This book can be ordered direct from the publisher:
- Pum Thai Food Chain Co., Ltd, 204/32 Rajuthit 200 Pi Road, Patong Beach, Phuket, 83150, Thailand +66 76 346 269
- Pumthaifoodchain Sàrl, 9 rue Louis Pasteur Mulhouse, France +33 3 89 66 39 74

For information regarding future publications, Pum Restaurants or Pum Cooking Schools please visit www.pumthaifoodchain.com or email us at info@pumthaifoodchain.com.

ISBN: 974-272-701-5

for my grandparents...

Contents

the story to tell

chapter 1

Little Girl

The story started when I was about 5 or 6 years old. At the break of dawn I would walk to the market with my Grandmother.

A little girl with her Grandma in the morning market, she would tell me of her childhood with Great-Grandma showing her how to buy vegetables, meat, fruit and so on (telling me something about food). I would listen but it passed through my head (sad to say, but I was so young). I just said 'yes' to please her. After the shopping I would clean, cut and help her to prepare food for the whole family (this is Thai culture, we used to live with everybody; Aunties, Uncles and cousins, one big family in one small, small house).

Around the age of 10:

Yeah! I started to cook and go to the market by myself and cooked for a very big family for many years, but I have to say that I did not enjoy cooking at all. Wow, very tiring!!!

A Young Lady in Cheltenham, England

I left Thailand for my education. I chose to go to England and I was very happy to leave the kitchen. I booked my accommodation (with food provided!) with my host family, Barbara & Derek. Yippee....no more cooking, I was so pleased not having to cook and I did not miss Thai food. I love eating and did not mind trying other cuisines.

Maybe I was too young when my Grandma showed me how to buy food, how to prepare and how to cook. I did not appreciate it much and just did it because it was my duty.

After many months had passed Barbara decided to tell me how much she loves Thai Red Curry.

Well I was so surprised when she asked "Pum, can you cook?" What could I say?

"Yes"...and I have cooked ever since...

6

London Life with the Stone Family

After Cheltenham I moved to 86 Kenilworth Court in Putney, South London and for the following year and a half I lived with the Stone family. They are my best friend's cousins and I was very happy living with them and got on very well with Jeni and Ray (Jeni's father). He loves cooking and his favourite was baked carrots. Very good for Christmas dinner and very yummy. You should try!

Many days were spent walking around the parks and along the Thames returning home to cook for my friend Reona whilst she played the violin.

One day Jeni decided to ask me to help her for a party. Well, I was so happy and said "Ok Jen I will do a very good spaghetti with red curry sauce". She replied simply with "wow!" And the party went well. Everybody liked the sauce but Tim, Jeni's friend, felt it was very spicy.

Well done Pum! It was my first big party in Putney. More to come...

8

The Story Continues

Later I moved to Wales the *'green, green grass of home'*, also home to good lamb, lovely leek soup and rainy days with Welsh cake.

Wales was where i intended to study and university life would be so cool if there were no essays and no exams... but again my 1st year was very happy because I had lots of parties and cooked every single weekend.

We all tried many recipes such as:

- Lazy Thai food from Pum.
- Very healthy and lazy tofu Chinese meals from Chi-hui.
- Grandma orange French cake from Sophie of France.
- Easy Spanish omelette from Juan.
- Quick starters from Mexicans Luis and Antonio.
- Traditional tiramisu from Busca's Cosmopolitan - the best and laziest.
- Steamed fresh greens African style by Madame Jackie from Botswana.
- Simple baked parsnip from Esther.
- 10-minute brownies made by Nao, a good looking Japanese lady.
- 5-minute microwave spinach topped with oyster sauce from lovely French lady Coco.

- Very spicy Indian fish red curry made by Bee Ee, my Chinese friend from Penang (I have to say the hottest curry in the world, it was bloody hot on earth).
- The best Thai fried rice with shrimp paste and clear soup by little Nong from Bangkok.

All this food was so much nicer than the soggy cucumber sandwiches we had at graduation ceremonies. It all went so well...weekend parties...cooking...eating...chatting.

The 2nd and 3rd years of university went so slow, more essays to do, and more difficult studies.

I just wanted to be efficient in the kitchen. Because I had no time to cook, I would just have a very quick meal, but not very healthy and it wasn't until my 4th year I started to think about good food for my brain. Without it I could not think about new theories for my studies. What is more, doing this difficult degree, I found cooking to be relaxing and beautiful which kept me happy and healthy.

The equation was simple; take a lazy person who loves eating but has little time to cook and buy the ingredients. How to feed her? Many variables, but one solution: explore lazy cuisine!

lazy cuisine

chapter 2

Lazy Cooking

Lazy cooking and staying happy and healthy are still with me. Why is this?

Nowadays people have many excuses saying that they have no time for cooking, preferring instead to sit in front of the TV.

It may be because they see the kitchen as hot, hard work and time consuming which may be true from the past, but if you follow my steps to cooking you will be very, very lazy, very happy and very healthy.

Be confident - students talking about their teacher:

I have been teaching classes of my 'lazy cuisine' since I opened my first restaurant in 2001 on Ko Phi Phi in Thailand. I have taught a countless number of students and the only advertising has been through word of mouth.

They all really make my day and give me more energy to continue. I have to 'krob khun ka' (thank) all my students, without their comments and support this book may not exist and their teacher would have no more power either!

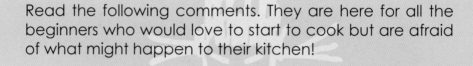

Read the following comments. They are here for all the beginners who would love to start to cook but are afraid of what might happen to their kitchen!

"One of the best classes in my life! You open my eyes for the beauty of the simplicity…"

14 July 2007 from Slovenia 'Anna'

"I am taking the lesson together with my daughter. It has been a wonderful experience for us. Thanks for Pum & the wonderful staff…"

7 August 2007 from Hong Kong 'Jessie & Peter Fung'

"Wonderful food still! We love using 'Pum's Lazy Cuisine' book, cooking Thai food at home…"

21 July 2007 from New Zealand ' Maxilyn & John Powen'

I just want to give you confidence from them. They were all lovely students. Some of them had never ever cooked in their life and I have shown them how simple, easy, colourful, sociable, very lazy and enjoyable cooking can be.

We all agree that these recipes are not difficult at all, the hardest part is getting the perfect shopping list (kitchen utensils, herbs, sauces, vegetables and all the remaining ingredients), but please don't worry, I will guide you to make this task as easy as possible.

Food is Art

Of course, everybody would agree with this statement. Preparing food is a way of communicating. The cook can express her feelings and what she wants to share with her guests.

For instance, the most significant part of cooking is love, it helps when you love someone and want to cook for them.

At work I have my favourite customers and students whom I take very special care of and put extra love in their food.

Eating is sensual. A dish speaks to all the five senses. Of course scent and taste are the most important, and the core of the cook's art is expressed in her ability to combine new ingredients to produce new flavours.

Even though many people think about the taste of the ingredients they forget to think about the colours and presentation of their food.

Both colour and presentation are very important to me because this is the first impression people receive about their food. If it looks 'soo-ay' (beautiful) they will want to eat. And to promote the dish's beauty a lovely smile and friendly service is the best advertisement. This idea comes when I serve my food to my customers and they keep coming back. Is it because of the food or because of me who loves talking? Well, it could be both!

That is why we need attention for our food in order to create lovely colours and tempt our friends and family. Of course the taste should be good as well!

"Cooking is a true art and teaching is a gift. You do both so wonderfully"

14th June 2002 'Dr Gerard J. Carvalho'

"Best food since we have been in Thailand. The décor & atmosphere is great. Would love to do cooking class next time…"

31st October 2003 'John & Lisa Deoley'

"It is not just the wonderful food, but the other details like the atmosphere, service, music, styling and the lemon juice is world class too!!!"

24th February 2004 from Sweden 'Pille Pensa & Jan Hedstrom'

Everybody seems to agree saying that cooking is a part of art: colourful, simple and served with lots of love and big smiles.

So, be lazy, but in an artistic way!!!

Simple kitchen

Remember that all my students think that for my lazy recipes the most difficult thing is getting the proper materials and ingredients. Indeed, as for any project, preparation is the most important step, but as I promised you, I will guide you to make this part as lazy as cooking. Right now, I am going to tell you how to prepare your simple kitchen. Let's go!

Cooking utensils

You do not need many specific tools, apart from a wok, a pestle & mortar and a rice cooker. These will all make your life beautiful.

Chinese spoons are very convenient for measuring your ingredients. They can be purchased in one of my restaurants or from my website. If you don't have any then remember a Chinese spoon contains 12.5 ml.

You probably have most of the rest in your kitchen, such as knives, a knife sharpener, chopping board, pots, electric blender, deep-frying ladle, ladle, serving dishes, kitchen dishes, serving spoons & forks, wire draining spoon and microwave; therefore it is quite easy to upgrade to the status of 'Asian Chef'.

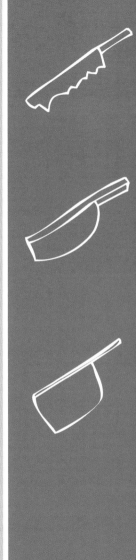

A few comments

- A wok is not all that necessary for the Asian stir fries, they can all be done in a frying pan because we are mainly using low heat; but you do want to look authentic don't you?!

- A rice cooker is a very good investment because it lasts a very long time and is very handy when we have to cook a lot of rice for the evening: the rice cooker will take away the worry for us! What do you think about this?

- The pestle & mortar are also needed for our curry pastes. The best way to buy one is to go to a Thai store and get one from there because they are well made and not too expensive either.

- Gas is better but electric stoves are fine. When we do all the stir frying or boiling we use a low heat (except for Phad Thai - Thai fried noodles). No worry!

- To make measuring easy, steal an old fashioned ice cream bowl from your Grandma. It doesn't need to be beautiful, just very solid, and hold the equivalent of 60 grams of cooked rice.

lady P sauces & pastes

who is lady P?

Using the right sauces is important.

They can be difficult to find and using the wrong sauces will be bad for your cooking, and you dont want to have bad cooking do you? So to save you searching I have done the hard work for you.

I now have a range of delicious and convenient sauces available to buy. If you live near one of my restaurants then just pop in and stock up or, if you prefer, you can order them online at www.pumthaifoodchain.com, just look for the Lady P logo.

You can also try making them yourself they are not too difficult to make and they will keep in the fridge for some time ready for you to use when you like.

Here are all the secret recipes (hush, for pity's sake do not tell anyone I told you).

lazy cuisine

sauces

Lady P Sauce
You will use this in many of my stir fry recipes, it is so easy and quick and will make your life beautiful.

Light soy sauce	1 Chinese spoon
Oyster sauce	1 Chinese spoon
Sugar	1 Chinese spoon

Lady P Sweet & Sour Sauce
Everybody loves sweet and sour but many find it so difficult to get right, this sauce will save you a headache!

Light soy sauce	1 Chinese spoon
Oyster sauce	1 Chinese spoon
Sugar	1 Chinese spoon
Chilli sauce	1 Chinese spoon
Tomato ketchup	1 Chinese spoon

How to mix
The method is the same for both sauces, simply mix the ingredients together until the sugar dissolves! If you find the flavour too strong you can add a little water to them.

Other Sauces
Other sauces such as Lady P Fish Sauce and Lady P Soy Sauce are also available but these are very difficult to make so it is better for you to buy them!

lazy cuisine

curry pastes

Green curry paste

Green chillies	20
Galangal	1 teaspoon
Lemon grass	3 Chinese spoons
Kaffir lime leaves (finely sliced)	3
Garlic (chopped)	2 Chinese spoons
Thai shallot	3 Chinese spoons
Salt	1 teaspoon
Thai sweet basil	1 handful
Vegetable oil	2 Chinese spoons

Red curry paste

Red chillies	20
Galangal	1 teaspoon
Lemon grass	3 Chinese spoons
Kaffir lime leaves (finely sliced)	3
Garlic (chopped)	2 Chinese spoons
Thai shallot	3 Chinese spoons
Salt	1 teaspoon
Chilli oil	2 Chinese spoons

How to Make the Pastes

The method is the same for both of the pastes; roughly chop the ingredients and then simply grind with a pestle & mortar. Remember to add the oil last so that you don't splash hot curry paste in your eyes.

There is no need to use an electric blender to get a smooth paste; if there are little chunks in the paste your friends can try and guess all of the ingredients and you will have a lot of fun talking.

They are easier than you think!

When you are ready come to my cooking school for the exam.

NB: Feel free to adjust the quantity of curry paste in each recipe in the book. Add more paste for spicy and less for mild. If you use a brand other than Lady P curry pastes, then replace the 'Chinese spoons' you see in the recipes with 'teaspoons' of paste, otherwise your friends may not be able to talk to you again!

chilli paste

Nam Prik Pow

Big dried red chillies	10
Garlic cloves	10
Thai shallots	20
Brown sugar	6 Chinese spoons
Lime juice	10 Chinese spoons
Small dried shrimps	2 Chinese spoons
Chilli oil	6 Chinese spoons
Vegetable oil	1 Chinese spoon

N.B: *for vegetarians just remove the dried shrimps.*

Roughly chop all of the ingredients and grind in a pestle & mortar and mix well. Add the vegetable oil and fry at a low heat until the oil turns red (do you recognise the 'chilli oil?).

Shopping Online

If you visit my website at www.pumthaifoodchain.com you will see a much larger range of products available to order online. They are all available in my restaurants as well.

More cook books, t-shirts, aprons, dishes and more, take a look and see if there is anything that interests you.

Happy shopping!!!

lazy cuisine

herbs & spices

Big red chilli (Prik Chee Fah) : about 3 inches long, moderately hot. For us the only use is for chicken satay dressing and lovely herb salad.

Big dried red chilli (Prik Haeng Med Yai) : the same size as 'prik chee fah'. Not too spicy and used in Thai chilli paste and Thai chilli oil.

Small red and green chillies (Prik Kee Noo) : literally 'mouse dropping chillies', about 1 inch in length, these little atomic bombs are very hot and very popular with the locals. There are many uses, dried or fresh.

Galangal (Kha) : it is a very popular ingredient of Thai curries and soups, a rhizome in the same family as ginger and turmeric, it has a zesty, almost piney fragrance.

Garlic (Kratiam) : many types of garlic are available, any of them are fine to use.

Kaffir lime leaves (Bai Makrut) : another essential Thai ingredient, these leaves come from the kaffir lime tree, a wild variety of lime with very fragrant leaves.

Lime (Manao) : we all know the citrus flavour of limes, lemons can also be used.

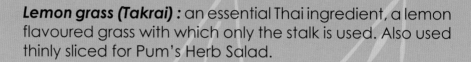

Lemon grass (Takrai) : an essential Thai ingredient, a lemon flavoured grass with which only the stalk is used. Also used thinly sliced for Pum's Herb Salad.

Thai shallots (Hom Daeng) : little purple shallots that have a sharp, slightly sweet flavour and are very good in Thai soups.

Thai sweet basil (Bai Horapa) : very popular with Thais and often used too generously (be careful) to flavour curries and also our 'green lipstick' paste. If you can't find Thai basil you can use 'ocimun basilicum' as a substitute.

lazy cuisine

sauces

Dark soy sauce (Siewe Dam) : darker, thicker, and stronger in flavour than its little brother. This is used sparingly to add a subtle colour and flavour to dishes.

Fish sauce (Nam Pla) : instead of using salt, we use 'nam pla'. The light coloured variety is better because of the good quality of the fish used and it does not smell in your house. Make up your mind please!

Tomato sauce (Sauce Makeua Thed) : we all know tomato sauce, some call it ketchup.

Vegetable oil (Nam Man Peuth) : cheap and healthy and adds no apparent flavour to the meal. Alternatives include corn or sunflower oil.

Vinegar (Nam Som Sai Choo) : the Thais mainly use rice vinegar, but it can be substituted by others.

Soy bean paste (Dow Jieo) : exactly as the name suggests, a paste made from soy beans. It adds an almost meaty flavour but is very salty so use it sparingly.

Chilli oil (Nam Man Nam Prik Pow) : bright red oil that is not too spicy at all.

+ = Fish Sauce

S + = Oyster Sauce

Chilli paste (Nam Prik Pow) : made, unsurprisingly, from chillies, amongst other ingredients. Very spicy so use with care!

Chilli sauce (Sauce Prik) : as easily available as ketchup, you will find them next to each other in the shop.

Coconut milk & cream (Kratee) : gives a lovely subtle flavour and creamy texture to dishes, best to buy it in cans if you can.

Oyster sauce (Nam Man Hoy) : made from oysters (not oyster mushrooms as my vegetarian friend thought) cooked with soy sauce; provides a salty, rich flavour to dishes. C'est très bon!

Light soy sauce (Siewe Kao) : it is absolutely essential for my cuisine. Pure vegetarians can substitute all the other sauces with this one. It is made from soy beans and has an almost clear colour and lovely salty taste.

= chilli paste

vegetables

Green beans (Tua Fak Yao) : you can also use French beans. In Thailand we use long beans or snake beans but there is no need to spend time searching for these.

Cabbage (Kalam Plee) : similar to your white cabbage but not quite as hard, you can use Savoy cabbage instead.

Carrots (Kerod) : orange things shaped like carrots!

Onions (Hom Yai) : many types are available, you can use any apart from the red variety.

Baby corn (Kao Phod Orn) : mini 'corn on the cob' or maize, about 4-5 inches long.

Cucumber (Dtaeng Kwah) : used for salads and soggy sandwiches at graduation parties.

Tomatoes (Makeua Thed) : use your favourite but only use the flesh don't use the seeds.

lazy cuisine

Chinese kale (Phak Kanah) : available in supermarkets but if you can't find it go to the Chinese store and ask for 'kaylan'.

Spring onion (Dton Hom) : also known as salad onions, green onions, new onions, scallions, shallots and fresh onions. Take your pick!

lazy cuisine

miscellaneous ingredients

Cashew nuts (Med Mamuang) : a nut with a subtle flavour and creamy texture.

Eggs (Kai) : from chickens, don't you know!

Large dry rice noodles (Kwitiaw Sen Yai) : made from rice flour. Strongly recommended to soak in water for about 20-25 minutes before using.

Thin dry rice noodles (Kwitiaw Sen Lek) : 'sen yai's' little brother. Made in the same way but cut thinner, also needs to be soaked before using.

Ground roasted peanuts (Tua Pon) : buy unsalted, unroasted peanuts then roast and grind them yourself.

Chilli powder (Prik Pon) : take small or large dried red chillies, just grind them up and here you have 'prik pon'.

Crispy fried garlic (Kratiam Jieaw) : fry 4 Chinese spoons of chopped garlic together with 12 Chinese spoons of vegetable oil at a low heat until the garlic turns golden brown. You can also buy it from any Chinese food shop!

lazy cuisine

miscellaneous
ingredients continued

Pickled radish (Tang Chai) : preserved white radish. It is easy to buy from any Chinese food shop.

Ground white pepper (Prik Tai) : if you are a beginner the black variety might make you think that you have burnt your food. I don't want you to panic or for your friends to complain.

Thai Jasmine rice (Khao Hom Mali) : please use this type of rice, it is very lovely.

Brown sugar (Nam Tan Sai Daeng) : unrefined cane sugar, don't use demerara or muscovado since the flavour is too strong and the colour is too dark.

Tapioca flour (Paeng Man) : used for thickening sauces, you can use corn flour instead.

Seems like a lot but the good thing is that both Thai and Asian cooking are very popular now so you should be able to find these ingredients without getting too much of a headache. Good luck with your shopping!

NOTA BENE: don't forget the meat of your choice, unless you are a vegetarian!

lazy cuisine

cooking time
...YEAH!

one more thing

Ooops!

I nearly forgot to tell you. All of the recipes that we are going to prepare are for one portion only. You can double the portions for two, but you should not prepare more than that in one go: too many ingredients in one pot and they all bang around and get headache, please don't hurt your veggies, they are very lovely!!!

- Cooking like foreigners: you would begin your meal with a starter, salad or soup, followed by a main course and dessert.

- Cooking like Thais: we do what we like, put all the food in the centre of the table and use a serving spoon for sharing. In that way everybody can try everything and tell us their favourite.

The decision is yours!

Let's start with...

starters

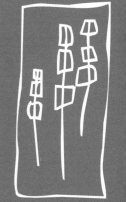

gai satay

Chicken Satay

Satay in not typically Thai. However it is popular all around our country, available in different variations with many kinds of meat used (pork, chicken, beef, shrimps, squid, etc...)

Chicken	2 handfuls
or meat of your choice (sliced)	
Garlic (chopped)	1 teaspoon
Lady P Yellow curry powder	2 teaspoons
Lady P Sauce	1 Chinese spoon
Vegetable oil	2 Chinese spoons

Mix all the ingredients in a bowl and then fry in the oil until the chicken is cooked.

Serve with the cucumber dressing and peanut sauce (see page 48)

cooking time

gai satay continued

Cucumber dressing

Hot water	45 ml
Cucumber	5 slices, cut in segments
Big red chilli (Prik Chee Fah)	1 inch, sliced
Thai shallot (sliced)	1
Vinegar	2 teaspoons
Sugar	3 teaspoons
Salt	3-4 pinches

Add the sugar, vinegar and salt to the hot water and stir until the sugar dissolves. Add the remaining ingredients and stir.

Peanut sauce

Ground peanuts	3 Chinese spoons
Lady P Coconut milk	4 Chinese spoons
Chilli oil	4 Chinese spoons
Sugar	2 Chinese spoons
Salt	3-4 pinches
Chilli powder	3-4 pinches

Mix all of the ingredients together in a saucepan and stir over a low heat until the sugar has dissolved. Pour into a bowl.

cooking time

gai kratiam

Chicken with Garlic and Pepper

Chicken (sliced)	2 handfuls
Garlic (chopped)	2 teaspoons
Lady P Sauce	1 Chinese spoon
Ground white pepper	1 teaspoon
Vegetable oil	2 Chinese spoons

Step 1
Mix together all of the ingredients except the vegetable oil.

Step 2
At low heat pour the vegetable oil into a wok and add the mixture from Step 1. Fry until the chicken is cooked. Serve with steamed rice and chilli sauce.

Enjoy your 'gai kratiam'.

cooking time

thod man pla

Fish Cakes

These are my favourite; I never get bored with them. Actually I need them to survive in this world! They are a little bit spicy and should be moist and tender. The fish cakes are served with the cucumber dressing (see page 48) in which they are dipped.

White fish fillet (cod, coley, haddock or monkfish)	2 handfuls
Lady P Red Curry Paste	1 Chinese spoon
Kaffir lime leaf (finely sliced)	1 leaf
Green beans (finely sliced)	2 Chinese spoons
Lady P Fish sauce	1½ Chinese spoons
Sugar	1 Chinese spoon
Vegetable oil	1 Chinese spoon

cooking time

Step 1
To make the fish cakes, mince the fish in a blender for a few seconds, add the red curry paste and mix again until it sticks together well.

Step 2
Remove the fish cakes mix from the blender and add the fish sauce, sugar, kaffir lime leaf and green beans, then mix well.

Step 3
Taking the mixture make balls with your hand and press them flat to make cakes roughly 5 cm in diameter and 1 cm thick.

Step 4
Fry at low heat, toss and turn until golden brown on both sides. Keep an eye on them otherwise you may get charcoal fish cakes!

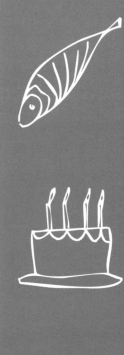

haw muk pla

Fish Cakes in Chinese Kale Cups

Haw Muk Pla is not really considered as a starter, but they are so easy to do after the fried fish cakes.

White fish fillet (cod, coley, haddock or monkfish)	2 handfuls
Lady P Red Curry Paste	1 Chinese spoon
Chinese kale	6 big leaves
Savoy cabbage (finely sliced)	2 Chinese spoons
Kaffir lime leaf (finely sliced)	1 leaf
Thai sweet basil	6 leaves
Green beans (finely sliced)	2 Chinese spoons
Big red chilli (cut as matchsticks)	1 inch
Lady P Fish sauce	1½ Chinese spoons
Sugar	1 Chinese spoon

cooking time

NB: when you buy your Chinese kale, try to get big leaves in order to make a cup (see the drawing)...

1

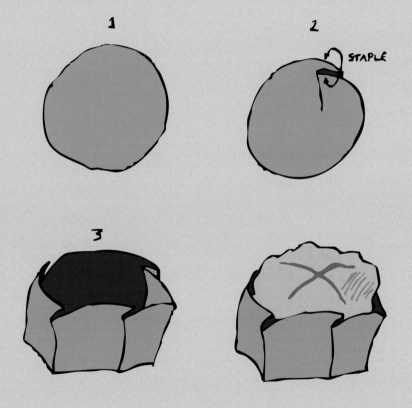

2

STAPLE

3

Step 1
To make the fish cakes, mince the fish in a blender for a few seconds, add the red curry paste and mix again until it sticks together well.

Step 2
Remove the fish cakes mix from the blender and add the fish sauce, sugar, kaffir lime leaf and green beans, then mix well.

Step 3
Put the sliced savoy cabbage in the bottom of each kale cup and top with Step 2.

Step 4
Steam the cups for 10-15 minutes and then garnish with the Thai sweet basil, big red chilli and the coconut milk.

pum's lazy dip

Minced chicken	1 handful
Lady P Red Curry Paste	1 Chinese spoon
Vegetable oil	1 Chinese spoon
Chilli oil	1 Chinese spoon
Lady P Fish Sauce	2 Chinese spoons
Sugar	1 Chinese spoon
Tomatoes (finely chopped)	2 tomatoes
Spring onion (chopped)	1 stalk

Step 1
In a bowl mix together the chicken, tomato, spring onion, fish sauce and sugar.

Step 2
At low heat in a saucepan add the oil and fry the red curry paste until fragrant and then add the mixture from Step 1. Stir well until the chicken is cooked. Serve in a bowl and garnish with a little 'red lipstick'.

Step 3
Serve the dip with fresh vegetables (savoy cabbage, cucumber, carrots or any vegetables of your choice). Very good for dieting! And if you are not dieting you can use the dip as a sauce for pasta.

salad
samunprai

Herb Salad

Savoy cabbage (finely sliced)	1 handful
Carrots (cut as matchsticks)	½ handful
Cucumber (cut as matchsticks)	½ handful
Tomatoes (cut in segments)	½ tomato
Thai shallots (sliced)	2
Big red chilli (cut as matchsticks)	1 inch
Kaffir lime leaves (finely sliced)	2
Lemon grass (finely sliced)	1 Chinese spoon
Garlic (chopped)	1 teaspoon
Lime juice	1 Chinese spoon
Vegetable oil	1 Chinese spoon
Lady P Sauce	2 Chinese spoons

Mix all of the ingredients together (adding the lime juice last) and serve.

cooking time

main dishes

cooking time

khao phad gaeng kheo wan phak

'Green Lipstick' Fried Rice with Vegetables

Cooked rice	60 g
Garlic (chopped)	1 teaspoon
Lady P Green Curry Paste	1 Chinese spoon
Vegetable oil	1 Chinese spoon
Baby corn (cut into small cubes)	1 teaspoon
Onion (cut into small cubes)	1 teaspoon
Carrot (cut into small cubes)	1 teaspoon
Spring onion (chopped)	1 teaspoon
Sugar	1 teaspoon
Pepper	2-3 pinches
Lady P Soy Sauce	2 Chinese spoons

cooking time

khao phad gaeng kheo wan phak continued

Step 1
Prepare the cooked rice in a bowl and add the sugar, light soy sauce, garlic, ground pepper and curry paste.

Step 2
Put the vegetable oil into a wok and at low heat add all the vegetables (onion, carrot, spring onion and baby corn). Mix them well for about 2 minutes.

Step 3
Add the mixture prepared in Step 1. Combine well and cook for 2 minutes (not more please!)

Step 4
Serve your Khao Phad Gaeng Kheo Wan Phak.

NB: non vegetarians can add the meat of their choice to Step 2 before adding the vegetables.

cooking time

khao phad 'andaman'

'Andaman' Fried Rice

Cooked rice	60 g
Garlic (chopped)	1 teaspoon
Minced chicken	1 Chinese spoon
Tuna	1 Chinese spoon
Vegetable oil	1 Chinese spoon
Pineapple	1 teaspoon
(cut into small cubes)	
Onion	1 teaspoon
(cut into small cubes)	
Carrot	1 teaspoon
(cut into small cubes)	
Spring onion (sliced)	1 teaspoon
Sugar	1 teaspoon
Pepper	2-3 pinches
Lady P Soy Sauce	2 Chinese spoons

cooking time

khao phad
'andaman' continued

Step 1
Prepare the cooked rice in a bowl and add the sugar, light soy sauce, garlic and ground pepper.

Step 2
Put the vegetable oil into a wok and at low heat fry the minced chicken and tuna. Then add all of the vegetables (onion, carrot, tomato, spring onion and pineapple). Mix them well for about 2 minutes.

Step 3
Add the mixture prepared in Step 1. Combine well and cook for 2 minutes (not more please!)

Step 4
Serve this lovely Andaman fried rice.

NB: for 'Fried Rice with Seafood' and 'Fried Rice with your choice of meat' simply remove the pineapple (substitute with baby corn or yellow bell pepper), tuna and chicken and replace with whichever meat you would like.

cooking time

phad thai - pum's dear lesson

Thai Fried Noodles

Lady P Small Rice Noodles (soaked)	1 handful
Fresh prawns	3
Egg	1
Vegetable oil	2 Chinese spoons
Garlic (chopped)	1 teaspoon
Lime juice	1 Chinese spoon
Sugar	1 Chinese spoon
Lady P Soy Sauce	2 Chinese spoons
Green beans (cut as an inch)	½ handful
Savoy cabbage (cut as a square inch)	1 handful
Ground peanuts	1 Chinese spoon
Lime for garnish	¼ lime

phad thai -
pum's dear
lesson continued

Step 1
Before cooking, soak the noodles in cold water for about 20-25 minutes until they become soft and then drain. In a pot, bring 1 litre of water to the boil. Soak the noodles in the boiling water for 3-4 seconds, remove them and place them on a plate (stand-by or réserver if you are a Frenchy).

Step 2
In the same pot of boiling water, quickly soak the vegetables (savoy cabbage and green beans) for 3-4 seconds and then drain. Put them together with the noodles and add the garlic, light soy sauce, sugar and lime juice.

Step 3
Break the egg into a bowl. Soak the prawns in hot water until pink and add to the egg. Mix well.

Step 4
Heat the oil in a wok until it becomes hot then add the mixture prepared in Step 3 and fry like an omelette. Remove from the wok and set aside.

Step 5
Place the ingredients from Step 2 into the wok and stir to combine. Turn off the heat and serve. Top with the omelette and garnish with the lime and ground peanuts. Yummy!

phad siewe

Fried Noodles with Sweet Soy Sauce

Lady P Large Rice Noodles (soaked)	1 handful
Meat of your choice or vegetables (sliced)	1 handful
Vegetable oil	1 Chinese spoon
Garlic (chopped)	1 teaspoon
Sugar	1 Chinese spoon
Lady P Soy Sauce	2 Chinese spoons
Dark soy sauce	2-3 drops
Ground pepper	2-3 pinches
Chinese kale (cut as a square inch)	½ handful
Savoy cabbage (cut as a square inch)	1 handful
Carrots (sliced)	4-5 slices

Step 1
Before cooking, soak the noodles in cold water for about 20-25 minutes until they become soft and then drain. In a pot, bring 1 litre of water to the boil. Soak the noodles in the boiling water for 3-4 seconds and remove them and place them on a plate.

Step 2
In the same pot of boiling water, quickly soak the vegetables (savoy cabbage and Chinese kale) for 3-4 seconds and then drain. Put them together with the noodles and add the garlic, light soy sauce, dark soy sauce and sugar onto the noodles and vegetables.

Step 3
Heat the oil in a wok then add the meat of your choice, stir until the meat is cooked, then add Step 2. Stir to combine, then serve with a pinch of ground pepper.

cooking time

raad nah

Fried Noodles with Thick Sauce

Lady P Large Rice Noodles (soaked)	1 handful
Water	340ml
Meat of your choice or vegetables (sliced)	1 handful
Vegetable oil	1 Chinese spoon
Garlic (chopped)	1 teaspoon
Soy bean paste	1 teaspoon
Sugar	1 Chinese spoon
Lady P Soy Sauce	2 Chinese spoons
Dark soy sauce	2-3 drops
Tapioca flour	2 Chinese spoons
Ground pepper	2-3 pinches
Chinese kale (cut as a square inch)	½ handful
Savoy cabbage (cut as a square inch)	1 handful
Carrots (sliced)	4-5 slices

cooking time

Step 1
Before cooking, soak the noodles in cold water for about 20-25 minutes until they become soft and then drain. In a pot, bring 1 litre of water to the boil. Soak the noodles in the boiling water for 3-4 seconds, remove them and place them on a plate

Step 2
In a wok add the vegetable oil and fry the noodles with dark soy sauce. Place on a serving dish. Add the water to the wok followed by the soy bean paste, garlic, sugar and light soy sauce. Stir and mix well.

Step 3
Bring the water to the boil and add the meat. When the meat is half cooked add all the vegetables and stir well. Add a little cold water to the tapioca flour and stir into the sauce until it becomes thick then turn the heat off.

Step 4
Pour the sauce over the noodles, garnish with pepper and serve this lovely 'British gravy'.

Bon appétit!

khao tom

Rice Soup with the Meat of your Choice

Rice soup was once a popular breakfast. Nowadays it is either found as a midnight snack after hanging out, or as a breakfast (after hangover!). It is quite simple to prepare and healthy to start the day with but Thai people now love to have an easy and simple continental breakfast or choose not to eat at all. What do you think?

Cooked rice	60 g
Water	340 ml
Meat of your choice or vegetables (sliced)	1 handful
Crispy fried garlic (see page 39)	1 teaspoon
Sugar	1 Chinese spoon
Lady P Soy Sauce	3 Chinese spoons
Ground pepper	2-3 pinches
Pickled radish (see page 41)	2-3 pinches
Baby corn (cut as an inch)	4 pieces
Chinese kale	½ handful
Savoy cabbage (cut as a square inch)	1 handful
Carrots (sliced)	4-5 slices

Step 1
In a pot, bring the water to the boil, add the pickled radish and meat together and keep boiling until it is cooked.

Step 2
Add the cooked rice and mix well with the soup and meat (or vegetables for vegetarians). Then add light soy sauce, sugar, pepper and the remaining vegetables: cook for 3-4 minutes, (be careful not to overcook the vegetables).

Step 3
Garnish with crispy fried garlic and serve.

kwitiaw nam

Noodle Soup with Meat of Your Choice

Noodle soup is quite popular at lunch for teenagers but also for Thais who work in commercial areas and have only a short lunch break. It is very fast to cook and healthy. I have taught my students, they found it very easy to prepare. Why don't you start now?

Lady P Large Rice Noodles (soaked)	1 handful
Water	340 ml
Meat of your choice or vegetables (sliced)	1 handful
Crispy fried garlic (see page 39)	1 teaspoon
Sugar	1 Chinese spoon
Lady P Soy Sauce	3 Chinese spoons
Ground pepper	2-3 pinches
Pickled radish (see page 41)	2-3 pinches
Baby corn (cut as an inch)	4 pieces
Chinese kale	½ handful
Savoy cabbage (cut as a square inch)	1 handful
Carrots (sliced)	4-5 slices

cooking time

Step 1
Before cooking, soak the large dry rice noodles in cold water for 20-25 minutes until they become soft and then drain.

Step 2
In a pot, bring the water to the boil, add the pickled radish and meat together and keep boiling until it is cooked.

Step 3
Add the soaked noodles and mix well with the soup and meat (or vegetables for vegetarians). Then add light soy sauce, sugar, pepper and the remaining vegetables: cook for 3-4 minutes, (be careful not to overcook the vegetables).

Step 4
Garnish with crispy fried garlic and serve.

gaeng daeng gai

Red Curry with Chicken

Chicken (sliced)	1 handful
Lady P Coconut Milk	100 ml
Water	100 ml
Vegetable oil	1 Chinese spoon
Lady P Red Curry Paste	1 Chinese spoon
Lady P Fish Sauce	2 Chinese spoons
Sugar	1 Chinese spoon
Green beans (cut as an inch)	½ handful
Carrots (sliced)	3-4 slices
Baby corn (cut as an inch)	4 pieces
Kaffir lime leaves	2
Chilli oil	3-4 drops

cooking time

Step 1

At a low heat in a pot, mix well the oil and red curry paste. Then add the chicken (or vegetables for vegetarians). Stir until all is half cooked.

Step 2

Add the coconut milk along with the fish sauce and sugar. Please mix them well.

Step 3

Add the water and vegetables. Bring to the boil and immediately pour into a bowl, garnish with kaffir lime leaves and add the drops chilli oil.

NB :

-   For vegetarians we should use only green beans, carrots and fresh baby corn - cut as an inch.

-   The proportion of coconut milk and water can be determined according to your taste; the more creamy you like it the higher the proportion of coconut milk (e.g. 150 ml coconut milk and 50 ml or water).

gaeng panaeng gai

Panaeng Curry with Chicken

Chicken (sliced)	1 handful
Lady P Coconut Milk	100 ml
Vegetable oil	1 Chinese spoon
Lady P Red Curry Paste	1 Chinese spoon
Lady P Fish Sauce	1 Chinese spoon
Sugar	1 Chinese spoon
Kaffir lime leaves (finely sliced)	1 leaf
Big red chilli (cut as matchsticks)	1 inch
Ground peanuts	1 Chinese spoon
Chilli oil	3-4 drops

cooking time

Step 1
At a low heat in a pot, mix well the oil and red curry paste. Then add the chicken (or vegetables for vegetarians). Stir until all is half cooked.

Step 2
Add the coconut milk, ground peanuts, fish sauce and sugar. Please mix them well.

Step 3
Bring to the boil and when the chicken is cooked immediately pour into a bowl and garnish with kaffir lime leaves, big red chilli and a few drops of chilli oil.

green lip

white lip

red lip

cooking thai

gaeng kheo wan gai - *green lipstick*

Green Curry with Chicken

There are three lipsticks in this book: green, white and red lipstick. I do like teaching these recipes to my students. They are very colourful and simple to prepare. However, 'green lipstick' is the most popular with my students. They love to make the paste and cooking it as well makes for a happy ending!

Follow the steps and enjoy my make-up!

cooking time

gaeng kheo wan gai - green lipstick continued

Chicken (sliced)	1 handful
Lady P Coconut Milk	100 ml
Water	100 ml
Vegetable oil	1 Chinese spoon
Lady P Green Curry Paste	1 Chinese spoon
Lady P Fish Sauce	2 Chinese spoons
Sugar	1 Chinese spoon
Green beans (cut as an inch)	1 handful
Kaffir lime leaves	2

Step 1
At low heat in a pot, mix well the oil and green curry paste. Then add the chicken (or vegetables for vegetarians). Stir until all is half cooked.

Step 2
Add the coconut milk along with the fish sauce and sugar. Please mix them well.

Step 3
Add the water and green beans. Bring to the boil and immediately pour into a bowl and garnish with kaffir lime leaves.

cooking time

green lip

white lip

red lip

cooking time

gaeng kheo wan gai - green lipstick continued

NB:
- For vegetarians we should use only green beans, carrots and fresh baby corn - cut as an inch.
- The proportion of coconut milk and water can be determined according to your taste; the more creamy you like it the higher the proportion of coconut milk (e.g. 150 ml coconut milk and 50 ml of water).

tom kha gai - *white lipstick*

Chicken in Coconut Milk Soup

Chicken (sliced)	1 handful
Lady P Coconut Milk	100 ml
Water	170 ml
Galangal (sliced)	4-5 slices
Lemon grass (cut as an inch)	½ stalk
Kaffir lime leaves	2
Thai shallot (pressed gently)	1
Small red chillies (pressed gently)	2
Lady P Fish Sauce	2 Chinese spoons
Sugar	1 Chinese spoon
Lime juice	2 Chinese spoons

green lip

white lip

red lip

cooking time

green lip

white lip

red lip

cooking time

tom kha gai -
white lipstick continued

Step 1
In a pot, add the coconut milk and bring to half boiling, then add the chicken and stir until the meat is half cooked.

Step 2
Add the fish sauce, sugar and lime juice. Please mix them well.

Step 3
Add all the herbs and wait until it boils. Serve in a bowl.

NB:
-   For vegetarians we should use only green beans, carrots and fresh baby corn - cut as an inch.
-   The proportion of coconut milk and water can be determined according to your taste; the more creamy you like it the higher the proportion of coconut milk (e.g. 200 ml coconut milk and 70 ml or water).

tom yum goong - red lipstick

green lip

white lip

red lip

Thai Hot & Sour Prawn Soup

Prawns	1 handful
Water	270 ml
Galangal (sliced)	4-5 slices
Lemon grass (cut as an inch)	½ stalk
Kaffir lime leaves	2
Thai shallot (pressed gently)	1
Small green chillies (pressed gently)	2
Lady P Chilli Paste	1 teaspoon
Chilli oil	3-4 drops
Lady P Fish Sauce	2 Chinese spoons
Sugar	1 Chinese spoon
Lime juice	3 Chinese spoons

cooking time

green lip

white lip

red lip

tom yum goong -
red lipstick continued

Step 1
Add the water to a pot and bring to half boiling, then add the chilli paste and mix well.

Step 2
Add the prawns or meat (or vegetables for the vegetarians) and let boil until it is half cooked. Then add the fish sauce, sugar and lime juice. Mix them well.

Step 3
Add all the herbs and wait until it boils. Serve in a bowl and garnish with 'red lipstick' (chilli oil).

Enjoy the make-up!

NB: For vegetarians we should use only green beans, carrots and fresh baby corn - cut as an inch.

gai phad med mamuang

Chicken with Cashew Nuts

Chicken (sliced)	1 handful
Garlic (chopped)	1 teaspoon
Vegetable oil	1 Chinese spoon
Lady P Chilli Paste	1 teaspoon
Chilli oil	3-4 drops
Lady P Sauce	3 Chinese spoons
Cashew nuts	2 Chinese spoons
Small onion (cut as a square inch)	½ handful
Spring onion (cut as an inch)	1 stalk

cooking time

gai phad
med mamuang <small>continued</small>

Step 1
Toast the cashew nuts in a dry wok for 2 minutes at a low heat and then set aside.

Step 2
Keeping at a low heat put the oil in the wok, add the chicken. Stir fry until it is half cooked, then add the chilli paste and garlic and mix well.

Step 3
Add the toasted cashew nuts, then add the Lady P Sauce and stir well.

Step 4
Add the onion, stir fry until it is half cooked. Add the spring onion, mix well and turn the heat off.

Don't forget to make her up by adding a few drops of chilli oil. Here is your lovely chicken with cashew nuts.

cooking time

phak phad med mamuang

Vegetables with Cashew Nuts

Garlic (chopped)	1 teaspoon
Vegetable oil	1 Chinese spoon
Lady P Chilli Paste	1 teaspoon
Chilli oil	3-4 drops
Cashew nuts	2 Chinese spoons
Lady P Sauce	3 Chinese spoons
Ground pepper	2-3 pinches
Small onion (cut as a square inch)	½ handful
Carrots (sliced)	½ handful
Savoy cabbage (cut as a square inch)	½ handful
Chinese kale (cut as a square inch)	½ handful
Baby corn (cut as an inch)	4 pieces

cooking time

phak phad
med mamuang continued

Step 1
Prepare all the vegetables in the same bowl, then add the garlic, chilli paste, Lady P Sauce and cashew nuts.

Step 2
At low heat put oil in a wok and immediately add Step 1. Mix well until the Chinese kale turns dark green. Turn off the heat.

Step 3
Garnish with ground pepper and chilli oil, then serve!

cooking time

phad nam prik pow

Fried Meat in Sweet Chilli Sauce

Meat of your choice or vegetables (sliced)	1 handful
Garlic (chopped)	1 teaspoon
Vegetable oil	1 Chinese spoon
Lady P Chilli Paste	1 teaspoon
Chilli oil	3-4 drops
Lady P Sauce	3 Chinese spoons
Small onion (cut as a square inch)	½ handful
Spring onion (cut as an inch)	1 stalk

cooking time

phad nam
prik pow continued

Step 1
At a low heat put the oil in the wok, add the meat. Stir fry until it is half cooked, then add the chilli paste and garlic and mix well.

Step 2
Add the Lady P Sauce and stir well.

Step 3
Add the onion, stir fry until it is half cooked. Add the spring onion, mix well and turn the heat off.

Don't forget to make her up with a little chilli oil.

phad nam prik pow phak

Fried Vegetables in Sweet Chilli Sauce

Garlic (chopped)	1 teaspoon
Vegetable oil	1 Chinese spoon
Lady P Chilli Paste	1 teaspoon
Chilli oil	3-4 drops
Lady P Sauce	3 Chinese spoons
Ground pepper	2-3 pinches
Small onion (cut as a square inch)	½ handful
Carrots (sliced)	½ handful
Savoy cabbage (cut as a square inch)	½ handful
Chinese kale (cut as a square inch)	½ handful
Baby corn (cut as an inch)	4 pieces

cooking time

phad nam
prik pow phak continued

Step 1
Prepare all the vegetables in the same bowl, then add the garlic, chilli paste, and the Lady P Sauce

Step 2
At low heat put the oil in a wok and immediately add the mixture prepared in Step 1. Mix well until the Chinese kale turns dark green. Turn off the heat.

Step 3
Garnish with ground pepper and chilli oil, then serve!

phad prio wan - united colours

Fried Meat or Vegetables in Sweet & Sour Sauce

Meat of your choice or vegetables (sliced)	½ handful
Garlic (chopped)	1 teaspoon
Vegetable oil	1 Chinese spoon
Lady P Sweet & Sour Sauce	3 Chinese spoons
Tomatoes (cut as a square inch)	½ tomato
Small onion (cut as a square inch)	½ handful
Carrots (sliced)	½ handful
Savoy cabbage (cut as a square inch)	½ handful
Chinese kale (cut as a square inch)	½ handful
Baby corn (cut as an inch)	4 pieces

cooking time

phad prio wan - united colours continued

Step 1
Prepare all of the vegetables in the same bowl, then add the garlic and the Lady P Sweet & Sour Sauce.

Step 2
At a low heat put the oil in a wok and immediately add the meat. Stir fry until the meat is half cooked.

Step 3
Add the mixed vegetables prepared in Step 1 and combine well until the Chinese kale turns dark green.

Turn off the heat and serve.

cooking time

phad phak ruam

Fried Mixed Vegetables

Garlic (chopped)	1 teaspoon
Vegetable oil	1 Chinese spoon
Lady P Sauce	3 Chinese spoons
Ground pepper	2-3 pinches
Tomatoes (cut as a square inch)	½ tomato
Small onion (cut as a square inch)	½ handful
Carrots (sliced)	½ handful
Savoy cabbage (cut as a square inch)	½ handful
Chinese kale (cut as a square inch)	½ handful
Baby corn (cut as an inch)	4 pieces

cooking time

Step 1
Prepare all of the vegetables in the same bowl, then add the garlic and the Lady P Sauce.

Step 2
At a low heat put the oil in a wok, immediately add the mixture prepared in Step 1 and combine well until the Chinese kale turns dark green.

Step 3
Turn off the heat, garnish with ground pepper and serve.

phad phak ruam sai prik chee fah

Fried Mixed Vegetables with Big Red Chilli

Garlic (chopped)	1 teaspoon
Vegetable oil	1 Chinese spoon
Lady P Sauce	3 Chinese spoons
Ground pepper	2-3 pinches
Big red chilli (sliced)	1 chilli
Tomatoes (cut as a square inch)	½ tomato
Small onion (cut as a square inch)	½ handful
Carrots (sliced)	½ handful
Savoy cabbage (cut as a square inch)	½ handful
Chinese kale (cut as a square inch)	½ handful
Baby corn (cut as an inch)	4 pieces

cooking time

Step 1
Prepare all of the vegetables and chillies in the same bowl, then add the garlic and the Lady P Sauce.

Step 2
At a low heat put the oil in a wok and immediately add the mixture prepared in Step 1 and combine well until the Chinese kale turns dark green.

Step 3
Turn off the heat, garnish with ground pepper and serve.

fish dancing under green lipstick - pum's special

Fish

Any boneless white fish	1 hand sized fillet
Garlic (chopped)	1 teaspoon
Lady P Sauce	1 Chinese spoon
Ground white pepper	1 teaspoon
Vegetable oil	1 Chinese spoon

Mix the ingredients together and coat the fish. Fry at low heat until cooked (about 2-3 minutes on each side). Set aside on a serving dish.

fish dancing under green lipstick - pum's special

'Green lipstick' sauce

Water	4 Chinese spoons
Lady P Green Curry Paste	4 teaspoons
Sugar	2 teaspoons
Lady P Fish Sauce	2 teaspoons
Oyster sauce	2 teaspoons
Lime juice	2 teaspoons
Vegetable oil	1 Chinese spoon

Step 1
At low heat put the oil in a pan and fry the curry paste until fragrant, then add the remaining sauces and simmer until the sauce is mixed well.

Step 2
Take the sleeping fish and top it with the sauce. Let the fish dance!

desserts

khao nieo mamuang

Mango with Sticky Rice

Asian desserts involve a lot of time and carving which is pretty tricky especially for lazy people (that includes me!). Therefore I have just one simple recipe for you.

Ripe yellow mango	½ a fruit
Lady P Coconut Milk	4 Chinese spoons
Sugar	2 Chinese spoons
Salt	2-3 pinches
Sticky rice	1 handful

Step 1
Prepare the mango by peeling and removing from the stone. Slice and set aside on a plate.

Step 2
Place the coconut milk, sugar and salt in a saucepan and heat gently, stirring until the sugar has dissolved.

cooking time

khao nieo
mamuang continued

Step 3
Remove from the heat and combine with the sticky rice. When mixed well serve alongside the mango and garnish with a little coconut milk.

Grandma's sticky rice
Soak the sticky rice in cold water for 12-14 hours and then drain. Steam for about 25-30 minutes until the rice is cooked.

Lazy sticky rice
Clean the sticky rice and bring some water to the boil. Simmer the sticky rice for about 10 minutes and then continue to steam the rice for a further 25-30 minutes.

Very lazy sticky rice
Soak risotto rice for about 10 minutes then steam for 25-30 minutes.

The very lazy way is working so well if you can't find proper sticky rice (very yummy).

cooking time

Enjoy your meal!

Are you tired?

Yes, I know you have worked a lot but now you get your reward...eating time!

"Mmm! Aroi dee!"
(impress your guests by speaking Thai)

happy ending

thank you

Sharing is the most beautiful part of my life, that is why I have shared all the secrets of my professional life from this book with my family, friends, editor, students, customers, readers and the investor.

I would love to say "krob pra khun mak ka" to my Grandma *Khun Yai Phaka Booranapim*. She is still saying "you have to stay happy and healthy" (in Thai language of course). Without her unlimited love, care, support and interest there wouldn't be lazy Pum's cooking.

Thanks to all of my many friends and a million thanks to the Slovenian family of *Maŝa Kmet* who have helped for this book by sending e-mails and kept asking about the progress of the book and also for cheering me up when I have had my rainy days.

Whilst experimenting recipes with the Grindall family, especially my editor *Josh Grindall*, many of my ideas (colour, presentation, simplicity, beauty and laziness) were worked out with him. I owe him and his family a special "krob khun mak ka" for putting up with me for so long.

My inspiration also came from all of my students who could not wait to read my second book. We had a lot of fun together at the cookery school (don't you remember your lovely teacher?)

Thanks a lot to everybody!

I get more energy when my customers say that my food is very tasty (lovely, unique, special, excellent, not too oily and very healthy); it really makes my day and keeps me smiling all day long. Thanks so much to all of you for paying for your food and therefore funding this book.

New friends, readers....welcome to my club and enjoy the membership. If you have nowhere to go, nothing to do, why don't you just pack your bags and come to visit me in 'The Land of Smiles!'.

The important person of this project is a business angel, *Mr Francis Flicker*, who has helped me from the beginning until the end of the project. Without him I would not have started the second book. Thank you so much for the right investment.

Lets cheer!

See you again for the third book...if you like. Bye bye!

happy ending

happy ending

happy ending

Noodle Soup

green lip

white lip

red lip

the key to understanding recipe names

Welcome to Thailand. The very first thing you should learn is 'same, same but different'!

If you do not understand the meaning why don't you come to Thailand and you would understand by yourself very well because I can't help for this. Sorry!

Thai language isn't difficult to understand once you know some basics. For the cuisine you need to know a few words which, when combined, describe the ingredients and the way the dish is prepared and that is the name of the recipe!

happy ending

basic words

Ingredients

Nua	Beef
Gai	Chicken
Moo	Pork
Pla	Fish
Goong	Prawns
Pooh	Crab
Khao	Rice
Phak	Vegetables
Med Mamuang	Cashew nuts
Prik	Chilli
Nam	Liquid or sauce
Kwitiaw	Noodles

Preparation

Phad	Fry
Tom	Boil
Prio	Sour
Wan	Sweet
Gaeng	Curry
Yum	Salad

Noodle Soup

green lip

white lip

red lip

homework

Now a few examples

Khao Phad Gai = *Rice Fried Chicken* : Fried rice with chicken

Yum Nua = *Salad Beef* : Beef salad

Gaeng Gai = *Curry Chicken* : Chicken curry

Now it's your turn to try:

Yum Pooh : _ _ a _   _ a _ a _
Phad Phak : _ r _ _ d   _ e _ e _ a _ _ _ s
Nam Prik : _ _ i _ _ i   _ a _ _ _
Kwitiaw Nam Moo : _ oo _ _ _   _ _ _ p   w _ _ _   _ o _ _
Nam Pla : _ _ s _   _ _ u _ _

Enjoy the game...if you don't find the answers then please write to me at:

info@pumthaifoodchain.com

or visit my website at www.pumthaifoodchain.com

120

My Photo Album

Phi Phi Restaurant

My Student

Pum's fish cakes
& sauce

Patong Restaurant

French Restaurant

My Students

Noodle Soup

green lip

white lip

red lip

happy ending

121

Noodle Soup

green lip

white lip

red lip

+ M = coconut milk

S + = oyster sauce

+ oil = chilli oil

happy ending

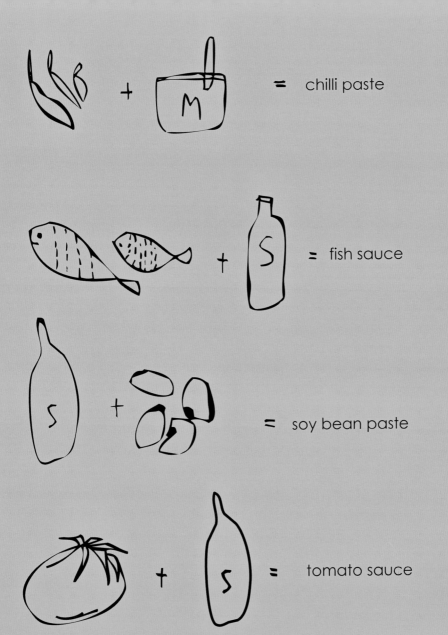

+ M = chilli paste

+ S = fish sauce

S + = soy bean paste

+ S = tomato sauce

happy ending

Noodle Soup

green lip

white lip

red lip

notes

Noodle Soup

green lip

white lip

red lip

happy ending

Noodle Soup

green lip

white lip

red lip

Noodle Soup

green lip

white lip

red lip

happy ending

Noodle Soup

green lip

white lip

red lip

happy ending